SNAKEDOCTOR

Also by Maurice Manning

SNAKEDOCTOR

Maurice Manning

COPPER CANYON PRESS

PORT TOWNSEND, WASHINGTON

Cover art: Stephen Hung, from *Dragonflies, Kenilworth Aquatic Gardens, Washington, D.C.,* 2021

Copper Canyon Press is in residence at Fort Worden State Park
in Port Townsend, Washington, under the auspices of Centrum.
Centrum is a gathering place for artists and creative thinkers
from around the world, students of all ages and backgrounds, and
audiences seeking extraordinary cultural enrichment.

LIBRARY OF CONGRESS CATALOGING-IN-PUBLICATION DATA
Names: Manning, Maurice, 1966- author.
Title: Snakedoctor / Maurice Manning.
Description: Port Townsend, Washington : Copper Canyon Press,
    [2023]
Identifiers: LCCN 2023017726 (print) |
    LCCN 2023017727 (ebook) | ISBN 9781556596988 (paperback) |
    ISBN 9781619322790 (epub)
Subjects: LCGFT: Poetry.
Classification: LCC PS3613.A5654 S63 2023 (print) |
    LCC PS3613.A5654 (ebook) | DDC 811/.6—dc23/eng/20230414
LC record available at https://lccn.loc.gov/2023017726
LC ebook record available at https://lccn.loc.gov/2023017727

9 8 7 6 5 4 3 2 FIRST PRINTING

COPPER CANYON PRESS
Post Office Box 271
Port Townsend, Washington 98368
www.coppercanyonpress.org

Acknowledgments

I am grateful to the following publications in which some of these poems originally appeared: *Appalachian Review, Cutleaf, The Eloquent Poem, Literary Matters, The New Yorker, Ploughshares, Plume, Post Road, Smartish Pace, South Carolina Review, Southern Cultures, Southern Humanities Review, Spiritus,* and *Time.*

for my daughter

CONTENTS

SNAKEDOCTOR

SUGAR

The boy had sugar, so every morning
he gave himself a shot in the top
of his thigh. I never watched him do it—
however, there was a fascination
and once, he let me touch the knot
of flesh that rose up, without
any wonder for him. He stuck
himself in the morning and that was that.
He also went to a slow school.
This is how he talked about himself—
he had sugar and he went to a school
for slow children, and these were the facts.
His father beat the hell out of him
for no good reason, but the boy
expected the beatings and learned to mark them
like notches on the stick of life.
The father used to joke he'd wear
the belt in two on the hide of his son,
if that's what it would take to make
the son follow the strict line—
Don't make me tan your hide, he'd say,
or, *I've a mind to give you a hiding*
and the son would cower and cry and shudder—
sometimes only a threat was made,
and that would satisfy the father.
I've wondered about the realities
of life, especially the things
that might be done in the name of love,
the unforgivable acts of love.
One summer my friend and I were playing
in the yard catching fireflies—
we called them lightning bugs—and let
them light a finger held up against the stars
or pointed to the darkness beyond
the trees at the back of the long yard.

A fire demon, a little devil
composed of fire with a fiery face
and black holes for eyes and mouth,
sprang out of a bush and ran beside us
along the ground and down the yard
before it returned to the spirit world.
I say *the spirit world* because
I've not seen anything like it since—
I've heard some haunted voices, but
I only saw the demon once.
We gave it a name, the two of us,
we decided to call it a fire demon,
because the world was literal
and that's how we were living in it.
A little blaze we saw just once.
He had a dog named Sugar, too.
She was just a big old country dog
who slept on the porch and never barked.
But she barked at the fire demon that night,
proof we had seen what we had seen
running blindly into the dark.
And Sugar always backed away
whenever the father raised his voice,
to lean against the boy's leg
exactly where he stuck himself.
She was just a big old country dog.
If there's a Resurrection for dogs,
she's one of a few I'd recommend.
The father lived with a misery
as old as the world and I think it broke him,
and the belt was just an illusion he held
and a sign of his own suffering,
and only in the allegory
that grows in the long garden of Time
can I see the belt for what it was
and the two boys and the dog and the demon.

4

You have to bring love into the world,
love, into the nameless world.

READING A BOOK IN THE WOODS

The spindly trunks of two trees
have twisted twice around each other.
This is what I see when I look up
from reading. I've read the page on the right
then turned to the left-hand page and read.
I've read the book all out of order,
beginning in the middle. Now,
by looking up, I know the book
is reading me. And there I am
in a middle chapter, whistling,
and knocking the back of my hand against
the motionless fruits of a hawthorn tree,
an action that has no consequence
unless the lifted hand and the branch
left swaying after are symbolic.
I could see it that way, but also see
how simple it is, how very little
is happening—no memory
is leaking out, no evident
signs of despair. There's sort of a dot,
dot, dot at this point in the book,
and I don't think the ending offers
much more. Maybe the sun goes down
and someone whistles in the dark,
or maybe it ends with pale light
still visible above the trees,
but we have been changed, and walk farther
into the woods and farther than that.

A CROOKED STAR IN PENCIL ON A PAGE

For some reason, I misremembered
a star someone made in the margin,
but there wasn't a star when I went back
to the page of the haunted, Gothic poem
that hangs in my mind like a coat on a hook.
Only a few words in ink,
here and there, to explain a passage.
One little fragment I like is this,
pessimistic about life. On the page
before, *gun* is underlined,
and later, a darker line is drawn
below *imagination*. It's strange,
but you can skim these notes, almost
illegible, and get the feel
of the larger poem and what the poet,
the younger one, was apprehending.
She—for I think it was a she—
puts it well in a difficult sentence:
Time is man's enemy
can't stop time. Being
a later reader of the book,
I put a star beside the sentence
this unknown reader made between
the stanzas of a poem I love
and drag behind me like a shadow.
As for me, I have no enemies—
I guess I disagree with thinking
I have an enemy—but I like
the difficult sentence, as sticky as tar
to say. That's why I made the star.

THREE LANDSCAPES

The Gospel of Happiness

One time, regarding happiness,
it came to me—you're supposed to feel it.
There are times when you're supposed to be
so happy you can hardly contain
yourself because you're overflowing.
And this is part of the whole design.
You see it in the sky, or looking
at hills billowing in the distance.
It also happens in the mind,
especially when you get the heart
involved, and it leads the mind along.
You can't believe the happiness
you feel, it billows over you,
like a wind in a book that's come alive.

Another time on a hillside,
and at a long distance from what
I thought I was seeing, I saw a leaf,
after the other leaves had fallen,
turning at the end of a branch.
It appeared by design to stir the air.
And then I walked toward the leaf
with a dull winter sky behind it,
unsure how I should understand
the symbol. Something useless and lonely
entered my mind, and then I saw
the leaf wasn't a leaf, but a wing,
and then I saw the rest of the bird,
the miracle, and was revived.

Greenbrier

This is a vine whose leaves stay green
in wintertime, and thorns stick out
to help it slowly climb a tree.
In bare woods it's like seeing a string
of green flags raised in the air.
The stubborn, heart-shaped leaves.
I think it is a lovely vine.
A blessing to see it in the woods,
high and silent and motionless.
Hillbillies who move to cities to find
a mindless job are sometimes called
briers, because they stick together.
And Greenbrier is also the name
of a place, a section of a county
in Kentucky where some of my people lived.
Every one of them is gone,
as though they never were alive.
But something of them is alive in me.
Maybe they've reached the City of God
and live in eternal light and joy,
or maybe they're just down in the ground.
I think I think too much about it.
But to name a place for a vine adorned
with thorns is moving to me, something
green and stubborn climbs in my mind.
To name a place symbolically
with the symbol all around—well, that
is deep, and there's some sadness in it.

The Moon Is Still in the Sky

Sometimes all I want to do
is go outside on a cold night
and walk in the woods. Let moonlight
glitter on the frosted trees.
Save the scurrying of the fox
through fallen leaves and the trickling,
twanging dulcimer of the stream,
may silence plainly speak itself.
May nothing be the mother tongue.
This is not my language and may I never
pretend it is for me to learn.
Make me only the listener.
  So we are tempted by perfection,
  the vision of possibility.

But the scene of the woods and the musical stream
and the glittering is not perfection.
It simply happens when the moon
is lighting the sky on a cold night
over a narrow patch of woods—
a haven of reflection burns
its lamp brighter, as in a mirror.
To see more clearly by reflection,
to be awake throughout the dream.
I believe in poetry and love.
I believe in the beauty of the woods,
how one becomes empty and filled
at once in the night-tuned silence
and the blessing in the glow is alive.

LICKS

We each were given three licks
for throwing snowballs against the side
of the school and making them stick. It snowed
so rarely we didn't know what snow
could do. Lessons were over but we
were lingering outside before
we walked the alleyway and the field
where our tracks in the snow would jumble together
and then untangle on our way home.
I had the farthest way to go,
but not so far, and a paper route
and other chores before the dark.
Homework was nowhere in my mind.
I was trying to make a face on the wall,
but it just looked like a bunch of blotches.
That was all right with me, though, I liked
the blotchy white against the brick.
It looked like several moons were stranded
in the cold universe of the wall.
The principal said we'd broken a rule,
but we didn't know the rule existed.
Our protest sailed over his head.
The principal said we were lying now
and he was going to light us up.
So, that's what he did, three licks each.
A horse in a painting over his desk,
where we had to bend and place our hands,
was supposed to wink with every lick.
Whipping a boy with a wooden paddle
doesn't always change his mind
about the universe or snow.
It wasn't exactly the plank of reason,
that paddle on which we signed our names—
a record the principal liked to keep—

and there wasn't much principle behind it
and it didn't even hurt that much.

MR. TRUE

My father used to drink a lot
and get filled with rage, but sometimes he'd fall
into a strange combination
of melancholy and affection
for complete strangers, fellow drinkers
who were having hard times, too—
harder—and he had understanding.
I'd hear them stumble in the door,
my father likely singing verses
from a heartsick, gloomy song,
and then this stranger would be in the house.
The stranger had nowhere else to go
was the reason, then my father would hang
an arm over the stranger's shoulder,
his Good Samaritan routine.
It was kind of pitiful to be
a boy and have this going on.
My father would wake me up to meet
the stranger. And the stranger would humor me—
he'd pull a quarter from behind
my ear, or pop the false teeth
out of his mouth and suck them back,
like an animal who could do a trick.
One night, a giant appeared in our kitchen.
That's right, and his name was Mr. True.
He was over seven feet tall,
there wasn't any trick to that.
I thought he really was a giant,
he could hardly stand up straight in the room—
he didn't fit in a normal house.
In the morning I found Mr. True
still asleep on the floor. His feet
stuck out from under the quilt, they looked
like a pair of fishing boats I'd seen

in books, missing the sails. Later,
he took me outside and set me high
upon his shoulders. It was higher
than I had ever been except
in a tree. I was a little sailor
perched at the top of a mast. And then
Mr. True teetered around
and dropped me on the shore of the porch,
and floated away forever. A lot
of my childhood was filled with sorrow,
as if someone had planted a garden of sadness
and lonely things were always blooming,
but once or twice it was magical.
I met a giant named Mr. True,
and I learned that taking in a stranger
is a decent thing to do, and you
can do it singing. Whatever torment
my father knew, he had a heart
for strangers and their suffering,
and a song to bring them through the door.

SNAKEDOCTOR

This is a dream, in which the love
residing always in the world
returns to everything that is
or ever was—even to you,
Marvella Hall, so tall and strict,
my teacher in first grade, who kept
a rabbit in the classroom
as I recall, and required I sit
red faced in my little desk
after some mischief of mine was found
and needed punishment. Moving
from shame to shame has been my life,
a lot of it at least. It's something
to mention, not a complaint.

                              You must
be older than Job's pet possum
if you're still stepping on the ground.
Of course, I called you Mrs. Hall—
Marvella simply suits the dream.
Your first name, whatever it was,
was extravagant, in a country sense;
I'm confident I remember that,
a name I expect you came to loathe
because in your lifetime and mine,
the country-world with all its quirks
and eccentricities and its airs—
now there's a word!—of aspiration,
has fallen short and receded. Although
it hasn't gone away in fact,
the countryside exists and people
still live in the country, but the country
is damaged, we both know that, Marvella.
And being from a rural place
has become, in our time, an embarrassment.

I worry it's now too late to return,
then wonder, return to what or where?
Are we missing, having gone nowhere?
Have we decided not to learn
the mirth and wisdom planted
like trees before our time on Earth?
Is there a summoning spirit left
in a song or two we used to sing?

A fidgety child is one thing,
but I know adults who can't sit still,
and people are afraid of silence,
afraid to walk in the dark and go
in the woods to find the darkness glows.
That kind of glowing is what I mean
when I say love resides in the world.
But you have to look for it, and your heart
must open its metaphysical door
and then the love swoops in like a swallow,
by which I mean the splendid bird.
Swallows boiling over a field
of daisies and thistles below a sky
that's yellowing to glimmer at dusk.
The mind approaches what this means,
this scene suggesting significance
beyond itself, but most of the time
it trickles down, below the realm
of memory and drips away
in the lightless cavern of consciousness.

I regret, Marvella, that I've resorted
to all this pretty language—not
merely a cave, but a *lightless cavern
of consciousness*. Yet I was aware
of the cavern even as a boy
and learned later that part of being

alive requires the cavern to grow
and then you go down in it to see
what's there.

              A misty field with swallows
silhouetted against the sky,
the whir of bugs, a living dream.
That's where I'm coming from, Marvella.
Not everybody gets it, you see?
All things alive and dead and dying
and rising to life. Is there a way
to grasp it all, the joy, the grief,
and see it all together, not
as doom or fate, but as a whole
complete and plainly unified,
and a way to be alive in the world?
I want this to be a happy vision.
And so I will it to happiness,
though I'm unsteady as the guide.

I made a note not long ago—
with your inner eye you're supposed to see—
a notion that entered my mind after
an openly symbolic dream
and I was going over it,
a meditation in the dark.
There was a spot in the dream, a patch
of shadow, like a keyhole,
but it was in the air with woods
around it. The shadow had something in it,
something that blessed me and told me to keep
my inner eye on the little patch
of shadow.

              Remember those paintings that show
the immaculate heart of Mary, Marvella?
Her heart floating in the air

with religious doodads all around it?
That's what this shadow made me think of.

I've called this poem "Snakedoctor"
because I found a dragonfly
elegantly dead on the steps
of a church I was about to enter,
and remembered *snakedoctor* was
the equally poetic word
some country people used to use
to name this mesmerizing bug.
Unmoving now, it resembles a cross,
an awkwardly disfigured cross.

I'm sorry, Marvella, if you think
I'm going to throw some mystical water
on all of this. It isn't mine
to throw, so you can put away
your prim and practical umbrella.
I wanted to make a prayer and I did,
in half sleep after the dream,
not for an answer but a question.
The only way I have to reach you,
Marvella Hall, is through a poem.
I wanted you to know that you are loved,
you are loved, you are loved, you horsy old woman.

WHITE OAK SHADOW HALF A MILE AWAY

for Charles Wright

One thing I hadn't noticed before
is a tree that's standing on a hill
nearby, and I had to climb a hill
that's nearer in order to see it. Declining
November light, a solitary
tree, and its shadow darkening
the hill behind it like a smudge
of India ink. And I saw the shadow
before I determined the tree was there,
a dreamy little paradox.
To determine means you reach the end
of something, but I don't think I've reached
the end of the tree. It's entered my mind
and I'll keep looking at it there—
a thought or two will come from it,
I suppose. The tree will leave a mark.
I'm fine with that. It's good to have
a tree alive on a hill in your mind,
and then to study the actual tree
to see if it has other aspects.
The tree must be an oak because
the leaves are still attending it
like a bunch of people who haven't been
let out of church. That ought to evoke
a Scripture or bring to mind a hymn,
but I can only summon the story
of Zacchaeus, who climbed a sycamore,
and I don't think that really applies.
But that's all right. It's nice to have
something to think about and not
know where you're going. You'll come back
to it someday and then you'll know.

You have to believe that things come back,
though when they do they may have changed.
I don't know why I said the shadow
looked like a smudge of India ink—
it's not like I have a special thing
for India ink. It's just an expression,
it's just something that came into my mind
and it seemed like the right thing to say
because the shadow looked like a smudge
of something that from a distance was dark,
that was made, strangely, by the light.

Everything is a metaphor,
even the bent-over heads
of grass that's gone to seed and the sway
they make, and the rhythm of the swaying,
devoted little emblems of green.
Sometimes I turn the washtub
over when I think a rain
is coming in, to let the rain
thump the bottom of the tub,
a nice, low, sleepy sound, depending
on the rain. I enjoy that kind of truth,
the daydream wanders into the light.
More often, however, the washtub
only hangs by its handle from
a nail in the barn and the tub is mute
except when it catches from the distance
the old man farther down the way
calling his cows home for the night
with a high-pitched *whoo* and *whoop*
and the open tub cradles his voice
and lolls it lightly back, as if
a hymn is being sounded out.
It isn't despair I hear in his voice,
but I like to hear the lonely in it
and how the washtub makes it ring.
An old man's voice and a washtub,
a daydream making its way to the light—
very particular instruments.
We might as well add a spicebush
to the scene and work it into the low
refrain, the thumping, low refrain,
depending on the ringing rain.

MOVING THROUGH THE HOUSE

I am careful not to make much noise
at night when other people are sleeping.
My moving through the house is slight;
sometimes I rise from the chair to reach
a book and see what someone says
in silent words and imagine the mind
that said them first to itself in silence.
Someone writing a book at night;
someone, later, reading the book
at night. This is an old house;
I will become an old man
in this house. Sometimes I leave my ghost
in the house and step out on the porch
to see the miracle of stars
turning in their wheel and wonder
if a man moving through the house
is still a practical metaphor.
So far, it is, it reconciles.
The house is civilizing, the man
is loyal, the book reveals a mind
refining itself for later minds;
a life is mended—nothing is ended.
The sleepers sleep in the provinces
of love laid out below the stars.
The cold night ticks in Time.
The man walks back into the house
and finds the book he was looking for.

WALKING INTO THE DISTANCE

Midsummer and the path in the woods
is dark. I cannot see its end
or rather what I know to be
its sudden fading at the fence
before an unkempt, lonely field.
I cannot see the other end
when I look back, midway
on the walk I've taken, stepping slowly.
There must be something on my mind,
but I prefer to notice how
the sugar maples have dispersed
themselves, the buckeyes and the beech,
and soon, though longer for me, the poplars
will tower over other trees.

The recurring dream I've had for years
is to imagine the great trees,
and I've imagined there might be
a moral purpose to such a dream.
Sensual, decadent beauty
presenting itself completely with bugs
for music. And a butterfly—
insanely flapping its dun wings
until it snaps back to freedom
from the harmless thread a spider left—
silently recomposes itself,
as if nothing symbolic has happened,
to float farther into this moment
that has forever living in it.

THE GOSPEL OF MUSIC

You have to thank the great beyond
if your child delights in birdsong,
especially a chorus of it
a dizzy crowd of birds singing—
warbles, chits, and caws ringing
through the sanctuary of the woods.
Although I heard the birds myself,
it was the little one who pointed
her finger to the budding trees
and pronounced the word she has for music,
composed of a pair of syllables
both beginning vaguely with Y,
with emphasis rightly on the first.
It happens also to be the word
she has for donkey and the plural
of donkey. And it's also the word
she says regarding the photograph
of an old-time banjo player
she sees at suppertime. She sees
the sound of a silent instrument,
and that's the true Gospel of Music.
In the beginning was the word,
and the word was music and birds and donkeys,
and God was a serious banjo player
with an inscrutable face, who said
to everything alive, *I made*
the world for singing. Now, you sing.

TWO SHADOWS

The little one belongs to her
and the taller one is mine, though I doubt
she knows the shadows walking hand
in hand ahead of us in the field
are ours. If I walk behind her, mine,
without a word, overshadows
all of hers, a magic I think she likes.
And when I walk at her side again,
the two of us return, a giant
and his long-legged little helper,
who's new enough to walking still
she manages a wobble or swings
a foot in picking the place to put it.
None of this beautiful, secret love
will last. Other shadows will come
along, and she'll see her own one day
apart from mine. But before those fates
arrive, I'm going to stretch my arms,
and tipping and twirling, I'll show her how
to turn her shadow into a bird
and rest it softly in the tree,
and afterward, when she sees a shadow,
perhaps she'll think of birds or me.

A FLÂNEURISH PHRASE

Just writing the phrase *a flâneurish phrase*
is fun because you have to put
that little hat-like thing above
the *a* in *flâneurish,* as if the word
is planning a little stroll. It looks
like a pretty serious hat to me,
not leaning over like a beret.
He's probably doffed a coat as well.
Perhaps Flâneurish is going out
to get an affordable bottle of wine
and he wants to wear a serious hat
to make buying a bottle of wine
seem more respectable. I don't know.
It's a free country. He might be wearing
his lucky wine-buying hat.
Flâneurish could get some hard bread
while he's out and a little hunk of cheese.
That's perfectly respectable.
He could tip his hat on his way out
of the wine and cheese emporium
and the little bell would ding behind him.
And then he could stroll back home to his wife
who has a musical French name.
They could have a little wine and cheese.
He could shower her with flâneurish phrases
and she could be impressed and wooed
and then she'd yawn and say, *Flâneurish,*
take off that goofy hat and come
to bed, let's go to bed, my darling.

THERMOPYLAE

It's unincorporated, but
there's a place in Kentucky called Burning Springs,
a few knobby hills and a stream
and the smell of rotten eggs in the air.
An unlikely place for paradox,
but there it is, mysteriously,
the ground is oozing paradox.
If it was ever the scene of valor
it's unrecorded, which I prefer.
I think someone shot a mule there once.
What's so impressive about a bunch
of people dying needlessly?
And we've sort of bent the rules when it comes
to valor   as with many things,
we've tended to exaggerate.
Isn't courage a private matter
that doesn't crave recognition?
And I've been getting tired of all
the classical allusions—they're too,
uh, classical, a little too
highfalutin for my taste.
It's funny, all the Spartans are gone,
and the Greek warriors devoted
to Demeter or one of the other gods—
outnumbered and overrun by the Persians,
who, ironically, are also gone,
along with Persia itself. Persia
is gone from the maps. It's hard to believe.
And the ancient city-state of Sparta.
I remember being very confused
in school on all the city-states
and who was aligned with whom and why;
they never seemed too civilized
to me. But I was a bad student,

looking out the windows at trees
and doing a lot of daydreaming.
I've always liked the civilization
of trees and the gray-green, hoary
assembly of hills, the wordless meaning,
the silent assent of trees and hills.

LIKE FLICKS OF FLAME

There's very little point in keeping
two yellowish red-and-black wings
from a moth I found disarrayed
in the grass. I could have mistaken them
for petals, but I knew what they were,
and when I picked them up the dust
from the wings left smudges on my fingers
as grainy newsprint used to do
when I delivered papers and rolled them
as I went. And coming home my hands
revealed a blur of backward letters.
The news was senseless. I liked to visit
an old woman who lived in a room
and had stories from the older time,
and then a priest who lived at the end
of my route. I believe the doors of Heaven
opened for both of them who are gone
from this world and yet still matter in it.
But maybe that's the point, to mark
a life that lives beyond the life,
and as you read it there you see
the life is also reading you,
who found at your feet the flicker of wings
touching in the grass and touched them,
and then you took them home to keep.

BLIND TIGER

In the middle of a gray field
notched into a hillside,
by fate or dumb luck, stood
the stoic windowless cabin
no bigger than a chicken coop,
with a shelf in front and a secret door,
and all you had to do was open
the door and put your money in
if you wanted a bottle of red-eye
homemade whiskey back then.
Nobody saw you coming or going,
and you had no idea who
was hiding in the dark cabin
folding a couple of dollars in silence
into the darker bib-pocket
of the overalls. No faces found
each other in a silent gaze
of recognition or shame. The one
in the tiger had a rifle gun
to be sure. I can imagine it all,
even the summer heat and the droop
of branches over the blind tiger
to give it a primitive, timeless shade,
but I can't imagine being there
myself, the one inside, or the one
who sneaks out of the shadows and back
into the woods and disappears
to slake the awful suffering thirst
because I can't go through the moment
and not step out of it in grief,
or sometimes merely disbelief.
An Old Testament birthright,
the people of the old book
of air and distance and stories heard.

The main thing I think about
is history and how to answer
Time when it asks me to answer it,
and whether my reply should rhyme
because the silent moment I'm
imagining has music in it.

PLANTING TREES IN GOD'S COUNTRY

My people sot down, they say,
two hundred years before the beginning
of Time, being kicked out
of the place where they had been, never
to prosper there, only to toil.
And here, in deep woods and on hills
steep and rugged and rocky, they made
a hill farm, not to prosper,
but, in quiet hope, to survive,
to plant in the ground and feed themselves.
And that meant clearing a patch of land,
cutting the trees, breaking the dark,
original canopy in violence
to let the sunlight reach the ground.
All for a little corn and beans,
surrounded by the first beauty.
If this was done unthinkingly,
without a measure of regret,
I do not know. I have my thoughts.
We have to live with ignorance,
even, painfully, our own.
We also have to imagine the past
and believe we come from it, not
to undo it, but simply to imagine
and therefore belong, by opening
the ground. And then imagine shade
in summer coming to this place
again and birdsong in the branches
of heaven-reaching trees, living
ladders stuck in the ground to give
the future another rung of its past.
The invitation is to climb.
One thing I know about God's country—it's all
there is, and it's supposed to be alive.

RANDY WOODRED

The elementary hand leans
downward and to the right, as if
the letters are sliding down a hill,
but Randy Woodred wrote his name
in the margin of a book to be
remembered, or to remind himself
how free he was to see himself
in a book called *How to Know the Trees*.
His name appears out of nowhere.
Maybe he thought knowing the trees
was a way of reading them—leaf-pages,
branch-chapters, trunk-spine,
root-words, published by
a seed. The anonymous author.
The geography of being alive.
Randy Woodred, the nervous student
who probably didn't have a mind
for metaphor. Yet he left his name
as if he'd carved it on a tree
in a book about trees with a green cover.

CRUTCH

That was another sign of not
doing something right, to read
with your finger following along,
and worse to read the passage aloud.
We weren't supposed to hear the words
or feel them coming out of our mouths—
if we read like that we were using a crutch.
I used to imagine a face behind
my eyes and there I could see a mouth
pronouncing the words and it made a voice
I could listen to. That's how I read.
And we weren't supposed to count on our fingers
so I hid my hands in my lap and tapped
on my thighs or the underside of the desk
as if I were playing an instrument,
but I was counting, carrying over
the tens from the column of ones, or when
I needed to add another 8
to 64 I'd tap it out
because I could only go so far
doing my times from memory.
There was something wrong if you used your fingers
to count, and most of the children I knew
who did either learned to hide it or
eventually how to stop counting.

THE GOLDEN TREACHERY OF POETRY

I've got a yodel and a half
another yodel inside of me,
and a verse or two of tweedledee
to run a possum up a tree,
or just to make a dandy noise
for occasions when I use my voice
as if it were a harmonickee,
and now and then I find repose
by strumming my fingers against my nose
and, humming melodiously, I free
the one-stringed banjo that lives
beside the yodel and a half
I keep in me and the verse or two
of tweedledee, and of course I save
some room for serious poetry
because I believe, my friends, in Beauty
with a capital *B* and Dirt with a *D*,
but a banjo in a serious poem,
or a poem searching for Truth with a *T*,
may cause the poem to fall just short
of perfection, or encourage the poet
to resolve the poem by claiming he
can do a convincing imitation
of a chicken practicing the art
of silence in moody contemplation.

FISHING WITH THE OLD LADY

I was thinking what would be the most
outlandish title for a poem
and "Fishing with the Old Lady"
is what I came up with. The lady in question
isn't even approaching old
and we've only talked about fishing
as something we might do some day.
It's good for contemplation, I said,
the last time we were talking about it.
I can see that, she said. So we agree
about fishing. When I think of her
I sometimes think of a lily pad.
That probably has some connotations,
and not unpleasant ones either.

EAVESDROPPING, EARLY MORNING, EVERYTHING ALIVE

When dew drips down from leaves
to land on other lower leaves
and shines them to reflect the sun
with such precision that the reflection
presents the brighter light, I conclude
when going into the world to see
what morning has brought to it, one may
be looking simply for something to praise
without expecting to halt in the gaze
soon so clearly going both ways,
and that will shine all of the day
and riddle anything to say,
even when sleep and darkness call,
and so when praising, praise it all.

PASTORAL

This is a poem dealing with simple
rural life. That's what they call
a pastoral in respected books.
I must live a pastoral life because
today I noted a crow appeared
as if in contemplation right
in the middle of a field not yet
awake to spring. So the black tone
of the crow nicely contrasted the brownish,
yellowish hue of the field. The field
was vaster because the crow was in it.
The crow revealed itself by being
either unaware or aware
of its presence in the vastness.
But the contrast was a living thing.
The crow reminded me of joy.
All of it was exceptional,
it was a very beautiful scene.
A scene that doesn't need meaning
attached to it, but I expect
a lot of meaning is there, now that
the scene is floating in my mind—
the field is in my mind, the crow
is motionless, he's like a smudge
on a piece of yellow-brown paper
with tinges of green beginning to show.
It almost isn't happening,
but from a distance and quietly it is.

FIXED IT WITH A NICKEL

When I was still in school, not quite
sixteen, I worked with a little man
named Floyd, delivering heavy goods
for the hardware store. About half the time,
he said, the devil had ahold
of him. The other half of the time
the Lord was the one who had the hold.
He'd get with one for a while before
the other one would grab him back.
Are you ever on your own, I asked,
not tugged or torn by anything?
No in-between for me, he said.
We had to go to Boneyville
one winter day, a long ride
back then, to take a foundry stove
to a man who I remember had
a porch with four or five tall steps—
the steps were steeper than a ladder.
The old man stood at the top and grinned
as we struggled with the dead weight.
The vent window in the truck
whistled all the way out
so we talked loudly, but coming back
we wanted quiet so Floyd wedged
a shim of wood behind the latch
and the whistle stopped. I hadn't thought
about that trick for years until
I had to fix a whistle myself.
But I didn't have a shim nearby—
this time I fixed it with a nickel.

A CACKALACKY YARDBIRD RECONSIDERED

An old ancestor of mine ventured
to one of the Carolinas once
in order to retrieve a rooster.
It was a journey there and back,
uphill in both directions, the kind
of going forth that leads to a tale
requiring embellishment, a grim
appraisal of the human condition,
and a perty little barefoot gal—
who almost swayed the author from
his task to bring the rooster home.
There was even a witch somewhere in there,
but the author liked to tell the tale
a different way each time, as if
he knew a story has to change.
He called his rooster Lying Tom,
because the author had observed
a rooster can't abide the truth.
Now, the man I've called the author was
indeed the author of the tale,
but he was in the tale, you see,
and so, the author of his fate.
He had a scheme that reached beyond
the tale—to travel far to find
a yardbird from the furrenest place
a feller ever could imagine,
and thus the chance to make a boast,
common in those distant days,
but sure to bring the company
of strangers curious to see
the fine-fangled preening bird.
The story sprouted like a seed,
and Lying Tom became a legend,
and the author got to tell the tale.

That was the reason, I realize
now, with the foggy wisp of time
twitching like a spider silk
behind the tale, for fetching
the bird at all—the loneliness
a man could feel, even at home,
even when love is all around.
This same old-timer liked to gamble,
I'm told, on the top of a coffin lid—
making coffins was his trade,
and passing out in one was not
uncommon, given that the cards
went hand in hand with imbibery.
And yet, he aimed to be redeemed
eventually—the Lord would swoop
from out of nowhere like a hawk,
or flutter gentle as a dove,
to bring the broken human soul
together again and make it sing.
His tale was always about redemption,
but no one ever sees it coming,
not even the author of the tale.
Reckon I'm on my way, he said
one night in the dead heat of summer—
I just don't know it yet. He smiled
and spread out his cards in the dark,
symbolically on the coffin lid,
about the time old Lying Tom
crowed in the day on the early side,
when stars were still high in the sky
and the hillsides were holding Time
like a ladle full of cold soup.
But Lying Tom was a useful bird—
he filled the air with invention, and when
you live in such a lonely place,
invention is what you have to do—

it gives you something to talk about
if any strangers happen by
and loneliness is in their eyes.

HAIKU

300 Days and Nights of Fog

If this were the scene,
Oh, how we'd come to love it—
blind, cold, uncertain.

Arriving at the Village of Turn-Around-Town

No one here today
or yesterday, save three ghosts—
two of them I saw.

Inquiry of Brother Paul across the Hills

And how have you been,
young man in an ancient shell?
Wake up and pray, right?

THE KNOT

I have a complicated knot
I won't untie that lives on a loop
of string with another loop twisted
or wandered through it, as if the loops
belong to each other but it's not
easy to see how they are joined.
My father tied the knot long back,
some year when I didn't know him
when I didn't think he knew himself
or me, or would imagine now
the moment of my study, not
untying anything about
the knot he tied that now outlives him,
and sits there living on the string.

The double loop, the knot, the string
he tied with purpose and made this thing,
designed, I think, for doubling.
What else to do but study it,
to see the silent hitch and sing.
Old Man, I see your hand in mine
and in it something rare and fine.
I like a hitch in the line, like you—
my little art is doubling, too.
And you were just a lonely man
with a string and a pair of sleepy hands
who made a knot with two loops through it
to remind me without saying so,
you longed for love and tied me to it.

THE LATCH

One sound, the click of the latch on the gate,
is like the clap or the slighter slap
of a hand against a thigh to declare
someone who needs to clear his head
is leaving. The smitten wren chatters
as I walk through rain into the woods,
the hillside choir-loft,
where soon I see in silhouette
another bird bobbing like
a cork on the upper branch of a tree
in perfect rhythm with the rain.

Shouldn't I, in the gaze of silver droplets
clinging to black branches, follow
the sky and lay my burden down
on the ground below these open rafters?
Again I've gone to hear the song
of mercy and here it is, the resound
of higher voices, note by note,
and I look up to see the score
of the sky is plainly open and I,
a wanderer, have entered the song,
and must be singing, too.

FEATHER PILLOW

for Alan Shapiro

My great-grandmother long ago
made from chicken feathers pillows—
at least the one I have in blue
and gray ticking—on the farm,
the homeplace we call it, near
the mingled farms and the country store
composing a village called Plato. She
was poor, but, I recall, steady,
more faithful than she was religious.
When locust leaves flutter down
in September I think they look like feathers.
Her name was Maranda. All of this—
I call it slow knowledge—and there
I lay, sometimes unsettled, my head.

TURNER

One morning when the weather was strange
and haunted following a rain—
I believe a fog had settled like
a thought over the field and the sun
that peered through it troubled the thought—
I remember saying to myself,
for no one was around, it's like
we're living in a Turner painting,
a haunted cave of melody
so indistinct, almost unseen.
As if a painting could convey
its time and also imagine a time
after, but keep the original time
to let it heavily hang in the present.
The point is, something in the world
is timeless, beyond the measure of time,
yet we perceive the timeless in time,
aware of its weight and of its passing
lightly like a song through a voice.
It isn't always beautiful,
the voice, the time, the foggy scene.
I said the fog had settled like
a thought over the field, but the thought
was mine. I wasn't sure if the scene
was beautiful. Something was ghostly,
the spirit of something not alive
was there. But maybe it was alive,
a spirit passing through the night
now lingering over the field.
The sun, as cold as a cat's-eye marble,
was out of place in the scene, but there.
We love the sweeter passages
of time, but never get it right.
The sense of time floating in time,

the effort to capture time in time,
in verse, in the ancient rhythm of verse,
not in my voice, but a timeless voice
haunted by a timeless voice
before it—rhythmic, keeping time
to the world of trees and fields and fog
resounding, as if a fog resounds—
that is the effort of my art.
Such as it is. It's a plain thing,
as plain as a field in early spring
with two or three blurry symbols,
composed almost completely of silence—
because it's there, the oldest art.
And that's what Turner painted: silence.

AFTER ALL THESE YEARS MY WOMAN'S DONE GOT VOLUPTUOUS

for the Lady of the House

Life changes, things come and go,
and things that never were before
delightfully appear. One thing
that pleases me, *delectatio*
profundo—to give it classical freight—
is what I'll nicely call *increase.*
A rich bounty now lies abed
and I have feasted on the spread.
Previously, there was a wiggle—
modest, comely—yet add to that,
in time's sweet passage, lo, a jiggle,
and the situation suggests a panting
painting, where, ah, the birds do sing, and
the beloved's less a little thing.

MY LEFT SIDE

My left side is kinked and painful
in the neck and shoulder, in the hip,
and that's the side for most of what
I do—in hammering, or raising
above the left foot a shovel
to move the gritty dirt from high,
upended ground and level it.
Or, to begin with stacking stones,
I start on the left to make a wall,
or move a wall already there.
Or shoring the barn, I begin on the left—
uphill—or when I sing, in praise
or from an anguish I can't let fly
like a ragged crow over the hill,
I turn my head slightly to
the left, because it helps me hear
the song and when to put the hiccup
in the voice and let it lope along
like a tramp, and sometimes I just look
to the left to see if something's there,
if the figure entering the woods
halfway through the heartsick chorus
with his left hand raised is me.

MISTER BLAKE'S SKIN DON'T DIRT

Because the vanishing point hovers
ridges away and miles in the distance
of gray-green oblivion
to illuminate on a nearer ridge
the white speck of a house, it opens
the mind to wonder beyond what is seen
and only dimly perceived. I like
this kind of scene—very little
is known, and yet it's decorated
lavishly with absence. Art,
before it's made, may be like this,
and art, when finished or left unfinished,
may be like this. And love, so long
in understanding, may be like this.
I suppose we need reflection, we need
something beyond us pointing back.
And perhaps we need to imagine a house,
no bigger than a dot on the ridge,
is the home of someone who spends the morning
or evening dabbling in beauty,
or having elevated thoughts
on what makes beauty beautiful
and how something missing is key.
And perhaps we need to look at the world
and imagine something that isn't there
and then imagine something that is.

THE RED CHAIR

Believing and being hopeful and praying
are sometimes not enough to do
whatever it is I think I need—
a sort of peace in the valley for me.
But it's truer to say my course goes through
the darker valley of the shadow.
And the shadow is proverbial,
of course, hard to describe, but the psalm
addresses it well enough. My soul
has been restored a thousand times,
but then it languishes. I get it—
nothing is easy, the struggle is part
of the so-called journey. The journey
must be proverbial, too—I mean,
it's not like I'm going anywhere,
just sitting in my silent room.
I sit a lot in a red chair.
I stare into space and sometimes
I don't feel anything at all.
There's probably something underneath
I'm missing or not fully getting.
But that's part of it all, to be
in the dark, unknowing. To be unknowing
is a biggie when it comes to faith.
I wouldn't want to know it all,
to have a vision so complete
you don't have any doubts or wonders.
Why I must suffer and impair
myself in order to feel the depth
of love is a total mystery
to me. I'd prefer to go outside
and simply be alive in the green
and weather. Oh, I can do that well
enough, and have the whole transcendent

thing, but then the darkness like
a specter comes to rest beside me,
twitching, and everything becomes
abstract, proverbial, and low.
And I think, ironically, it's dark,
it's utter dark, this thing I must
pass through. And thus the red chair
I occupy, from which I see
the world and am involved in love.
I'm so involved with love it's hard
to fathom, hard to tell how much.
From my perspective, my love for the world
does not have end and has no measure.
There is no poetry in that
or a man sitting in a red chair.

RAIN

I really don't like going into
my own mind to sit there alone
with my so-called thoughts, my wonderings,
my four or five or however many
now it is griefs I can never explain
or resolve, if all I do is fiddle
around thinking I have an idea
or now know what to say about something.
I'd rather go out of my mind to let
something else come in, like rain,
and the sound of rain splattering
on leaves in the sanity of the woods
where nothing is alone, not even
the rackety wren, the real creation.

THE PENCIL LEAD IN MY FATHER'S FINGER

It was a little bluish dot
stuck in the ring-finger knuckle
of his right hand, and left there by
a boy from early school days,
whom I imagine now is also
dead and mostly gone from the world,
unless there are those whose memory
of the boy from the later 1930s'
hillside-violent-Kentucky
keeps something of that boy alive.
It wasn't an accident, the stab.
The boy was fighting, my father said,
when I myself a boy had asked
about the dot of blue stuck in
his finger, and he told me the story
behind the dot. I can't remember
all of it now, but I can see
the dot, a bluish spot in the finger
that isn't in the world at all.

ART

I have a leaf spring, sprung
like a rib from its cast-iron cage,
that hangs by crude design from a chain
and a piece of wire and a broken half
of a horseshoe. The other end
of the chain hangs from a hook at the end
of a long iron rod, out of
kilter, whose other end is stabbed
resolutely into the ground.
The whole contrivance, if you can now
imagine it, resembles a child's
invention of a suspension bridge
to join one realm of air to another.
Two nothings held together,
though sometimes turning in the wind,
or swaying when a bird lights on
the mute slat, and once again
it bounces, recalling its first design—
to cushion the buckboard bench
as the wagon rolled on down the road,
and the man sitting there was half
asleep under the cold blue stars,
but the rocks in the road yet gave some light
and the horse, whose name was Jupiter,
exactly knew the way to go,
he'd been so many times before,
parting the lonesome night in two
like a vein running through a leaf,
after the man had nodded off
and the last refrain of the song he liked
to sing about a woman's slippers
had left the air. Imagination
and memory, with real things
and two nothings strangely assembled,

part of a song, and the lonely dream
of being alive in a place on earth.

A PENITENTIARY ROCKING CHAIR

for Robert Boswell

I don't know what he was guilty of,
the little man who made the chair
back in the nineteenth-century
workshop with vises and blocks
and iron hoops for bending the arms,
a drowsy guard perched on a stool
made by prisoners as well,
and outside the timeless river
rolling along before being
swallowed by the Father of Waters,
the Indian name for the muddy heart
of the country. The ladder-back is long
and receives the back of the sitter's head
serenely. The elemental rocking
continues in the maw of Time,
and the hearth fire dazzles the room.
I went to the prison as a boy
to see the yellow electric chair—
it had a nickname I forget—
and later there's a photograph
of me perched on the lip of the pit
nearby and behind, as if preserved
in a permanent past, is the steam shovel,
the famous, one-of-a-kind machine,
as tall as the Statue of Liberty
and taller, that soon outlived its life
of growing ever underground
and, lurching over, it buried itself.
The dead machinery of death.
The chair creaks and I watch the fire
to imagine this keyhole dot
of Time. Light from the other side

is peeking through and the room is lit.
The little man back there is still
alive with his sleeves rolled up.
A tiny nail had worked its way
out of the wood but I tacked it back.
Poplar slats and hickory stretchers,
light as a feather and sturdy strong.
The language to describe this thing
made by a man forever unknown.
The vision to imagine him
while rocking in the chair he made,
arms on the arms embracing me,
and a question thought though not uttered,
about freedom and what it means,
and then the image of the river
comes to mind and the silence of it,
and not the irony of history,
but the plain, unyielding irony of Time.

THE DAYTIME GHOST

Sometimes I hear a squeaking sound
coming from the barn, a raspy mixture
of old wood and metal, like
a block and tackle that isn't there
hoisting something that isn't there,
the sound of a weightless thing in motion.
I've even been convinced to enter
the barn and look around—the design,
the labor of those gone from the Earth,
and the lamp of light that lit a mind—
to see if something else is there.
The man who lived here before me
was lean and stuttered and barely lived
in the world. He lived in another world,

with the mules he trained and plowlines
and the gleaming iron-faced plow
polished by moving through the ground.
I could have done that kind of work
and imagine the satisfaction of it,
to get the field just right and hope
the lines stay lines and don't wash out,
and in the end provide. The dream
I have is of obedience,
to get behind the plow and hear
my voice sing out to the mules.
That is the man I might have been,
but I'm not finished with him yet,
and he's not finished yet with me.

SINNER MAN

Imagining someone I never knew
is an obligation I have to Time,
and my experience of Time
is tied to undulating hills
with smoke and mist like froth on them
and therefore Time is in the World
and Time is in the stories I
as a boy was told from memory,
but the stories were not the story of Time.
Recalling in order to recreate
a story never fully told—
only in disconnected fragments—
is what I have to do with Time.
Yet Time is a stream with no beginning,
yet there are events that seem to be
in my assembly, original,
as in originating what
came after and how it came to me
and what I have to do about it.
The story of the story of Time—
the dog on the porch is still there
in the past, in the past light of the sun,
the chinking between the logs is gleaming
from whitewash, two horses
graze in the shade. The boy who was
my father is plowing with a mule.
The Time ahead is invisible
and swallowed in the timeless hills.
I could dream this all the way to Heaven
and lay it at the foot of God,
but that would contradict the facts.
The particular man I am obliged
to imagine is my father's father.
I've been told he was musical. He could sing

and pick up any instrument
with strings and turn it into a bird.
He must have had a gentle side,
if that was the sort of talent he had.
But, clearly, he had another side.
He shot two men in '38,
apparently in self-defense,
though with some measure of intent.
You could see the lint fly off their clothes
when the bullets hit, a detail someone
who was there reported to my father
and many years later he told me.
And then he shot another man
in '39, apparently
to settle the feud, and bend the rest
of his life with guilt and shame and what
I imagine must have felt like doom.
I would have liked to hear his voice.
Was it animated or resigned?
Was he a gentle, defeated man,
or did he live with raging rage?
He was known as Uncle Zeke by some,
though I didn't know that for forty years,
though to my father he was Daddy,
and a measure of shame was passed to him.
A different kind of shame, perhaps.
You get together men and guns
and red-eye whiskey and you'll have trouble
because the men in that condition
no longer see tomorrow, they can't
imagine anything but now—
and then they have to live that way
until the painful end and the pain
for him was treated with moonshine and morphine
and half his face had been cut away
by doctors who were trying to help,

and his death was allegorical
for its misery, as if guilt destroyed him,
and the reason I imagine him
is because he must have needed love
and was too hell-bent to ask for it.
And how can you live in the world like that?
The answer, Sinner Man, you can't.
The hillbilly habit is,
if the history books are right, to fight—
over a woman or wounded pride
or an egg-sucking dog or the law
not acting right or a dirty deal
or a stranger eyeing one of your own
or someone tromping on your place
or the schoolteacher switching your child
or the sun coming up somehow wrong
and there's nothing else to do but fight.
It's in the blood, it's in the blood,
a loyalty to take care of your own.
Even if they go wrong, you defend them—
you love them because they are your own.
And when the prodigal returns
the men slink off and get drunk
and the women praise the Lord he's home.
Eating the occasional possum
is also part of the routine,
and slinging up a hog in the fall
to let the blood drain in the bucket.
Do you hear this four-beat line I've got
clinging and clanging roughly along,
reader, out there in the lonely world?
I think I got it from him, my father's
father, whose voice I never heard,
not a single syllable or word,
but imagine what it sounded like—
he gave me something after all.

Damn the shame and damn the guilt.
Rise up, Old Man, and come to freedom.

THE DRAW

Bird hunting with my cousin
forty years ago in mild
fall weather, he looked out on
a scrubby patch in the woods and said,
Let's let the dog work up this draw
and see if she won't flush a bird.
He called it a draw, a little wrinkle
in the earth, wounded looking and stippled
with saw briars and vines, and a tree
bent by a wind or fate pitched
itself, as though in grief, at the head.
The dog flushed a bird all right,
she flushed two, but too far from
the great hunters to be in range.
That was a problem with the dog,
she went ahead of us too far.
I didn't want to shoot a bird
anyway, I was scared if I shot one
a heavy guilt would fall upon me
from the heavens or wherever guilt
is stored up like mystical treasure.
But that was a guilt that didn't fall.
I probably would have called the draw
a gulley, but I accepted the name
my cousin gave it because he knew
the world in ways that I did not
and with a word he taught me what
there is to learn about the world
and how one learns it by being in it,
the lesson of being briefly a hunter.
The birds with the grace of their design
flushed and flew off to the distance
perhaps to another draw somewhere.
I can see them flying even now

in their own eternity of grace,
and I can see the dog, her blunt
tail ticking as she nears
the fated tree and the head of the draw.

BLUE HOLE

There are places in streams and little rivers
where the current slows and the water is deeper
and someone decided to call these holes.
Well, that's the local name I know.
A hole in a little river or stream,
a hole you can see in water. Somewhere
in a photograph I have, my father's
father is holding a stringer of fish.
It's late in the 1930s I guess,
my father as a boy is standing
on a splay of rocks above a shoal.
There must be thirty fish on the stringer.
They'd been to the hole that day. In fact,
they called it a blue hole, because
the water was bluish-green. It was down
on Redbird. I like the grammar
of that particular phrase. It was down
on Redbird, that day back then
when they found a blue hole and the hole
created by Time was full of fish.
Down on Redbird. The water
over your head but you could see
right down to the bottom of the hole.
A river named for an Indian
supposedly kind to settlers.
That's the legend. You can also see
in the background some scraggly trees.
The bank looks low, an easy way
to get to the water. Nobody
in the picture knew what was going
to happen, but another kind
of hole was coming. It wasn't blue,
and it would swallow everyone
standing in the photograph taken

down on Redbird that day,
a hole not made by Time but by
the son of man, living in Time
and lost in the blur of Time and grief
and no one was coming back from it
because it doesn't have a bottom.
This is a meditation on language,
geography, and something else,
something that doesn't have a name.
By son of man, I mean the man
who's stretching the stringer of fish before him
like a grin, and isn't saying a thing,
though my father often said to me,
I wish you could have heard him sing.

A GENUINE DAVY CROCKETT COONSKIN CAP

Somewhere in there, in the early years,
it was important for me to get
to Tennessee, where I knew I could
acquire for my adventuring mind
a symbol of my desire for adventure
and my wilderness imaginings—
a symbol I thought would make them true,
a genuine Davy Crockett
Coonskin Cap. I was enthralled
by the history and what is now
regarded as a myth. So be it.
It mattered to the boy I was.
I didn't know the cap was made
of rabbit fur or the tail was fake.

HAY RAKE

The seat was big enough for two
and my feet couldn't reach the rests
and the reins were invisible when I jerked
them in the air and lightly clucked
to persuade the imaginary horse
to make his way into the field
and rake the imaginary hay
first into rows and then into ricks.
There was a lever to the right
and a few notches in a wheel
to let the rib cage of tines
lightly reach the ground and rake
the hay, though only rusted iron
by now, the lever was only a thing
I pretended to move. I pretended
my way all over the field, and then
I pretended to have a barn to fill,
but the old equipment didn't move.
And the field was just a patch of ground
with briers where a fence had been.
Sometimes if the ground was dry
I'd crawl into the tunnel of tines
and look up at the sky, or pretend
it was now the third hot day
and all I was was a field of hay.

PAINTING

If you look at some of the old paintings
where someone is gazing out with a blank
or nondescript expression, I think
the painter was wanting to express
an idea and not the person or
the spotless virtue of the person.
This really doesn't bother me,
but when you see in a painting someone
whose eyes are closed because he's blinking,
you tend to think that's pretty honest,
to see a human being that way,
and you also think the person there
was not the kind to sit around
all day and mope or overly sigh
and pretend to be brooding out the window,
with a vase of droopy flowers placed
on the sill to magnify the brooding.
There might be a lemon cut in two
on a board with one of the halves turned up
to symbolize longing, as if
it's believable that someone would cut
a lemon in two and leave it sitting
expressively on a windowsill.
If I were a painter I'd make the eyes
a little clouded over because
I'd want to indicate someone
seeing something he couldn't see
in reality. And I'd take away
the window and the windowsill.
There wouldn't be a place for the vase
or the weirdly sensual lemon. I'd put
the old man outside with a haze of trees
behind him and above the trees
I'd paint a significant patch of sky.

I'd paint it blue, but darken it,
to make it not quite clear if the man
is going to sleep or if he's drinking
the dew—or if he's just content
to stare into the world at night
and not be worrying about
his life or looking back on it.
He might be waiting for the moon.
A lot of people like looking
at the moon, or how it illuminates
a haze of trees and leaves a glow.
It's hard to complain about a glow.
I just don't think a painting needs
to be extravagant or dire
in order to be beautiful.

AS PLUCKING BLACKBERRIES IN THE FACE

As plucking blackberries in the face
of a sullen praying mantis—Oh, dalliance
between hand and the mystic pose!—so holiness
deprives the one who lives by hunger—though the fruit
may bruise, and the fingers blindly reaching out
may come back pricked by thorns, or love.

AFTER READING CHARLES WRIGHT, I TURN OUT
THE LIGHT AND LISTEN TO THE RAIN

Protestant American darkness
is always worldly, beginning in failure,
a failure that deepens in time to acquire
a punishing weight that can't be shaken.
Though it's always failure in worldly terms—
the material way to the easy life
falls short, the good times don't last.
No thought of living beyond the life
within the span of the living life.
And then the melancholy turn,
the great American illusion,
inert, nothing living in it,
unless you think despair is alive.

       Darkness according to the Eastern
beliefs I've casually encountered
is not as absolute. If you don't
quite make the illuminated tree
you can settle for the shadow behind it.
At least it's calm in such a shade,
a deep shadow, like being asleep.
I could live with the deep shadow approach.
Eastern enlightenment, I've noted,
doesn't need to be as bright.
The symbolic mountain is calmly cold
and usually shrouded in a mist.
A rain has tossed the blossoms down
though a few remain on the dark branch—
the watercolor is washed out.

In the West we like a golden explosion—
enlightenment is a spectacle,
and not connected to anything,
an anomaly that's just for us.

Mountains and valleys and long views,
the dead veins of a dropped leaf;
distances, the calliope music
of birds, silence, and slow time.

I've wanted to believe that art
and life could share a common purpose—
the aesthetic implying the ethical,
a way of being and going on.
I could be wrong about that. We'll see.
I know I have to loosen my lines.
And stop drowning the inexplicable
sorrows in order to clarify
the ditty that drifts down to the page.
None of that is important. Let
them go, forever unexplained.
And I must free myself from the left
margin to let the line float
alive, symbolically, back and forth
or out of sight, like a leaf in water.
The figure, the phrase, alive to its own
                motion, entwined with the other motion
                        below, or popping up in the water
                                somewhere approaching the other side.
                                        Whatever is on the other side.
                                                Something
                        defining the space around it,
                                even an awkward, absent
                space.

It looks like a dropped line to me—
I still can't do it unconsciously,
and still can't break it all apart
on purpose to leave the sense of meaning
behind. And so more learning, more reading,
more sitting alone, though not alone,
the opposite of alone, in fact.
You go beyond yourself to find
the place—vast or intimate
or both—where you belong and yet
remain unknown, merely dissolved
in the cosmic, watery hum of the place,
a serenity sometimes known in the world,
and the verse becomes about the place
and the hush of belonging to it all.
There's no point in doing any of this
if all you're going to do is complain.
Anger stiffens everything.
What a waste of time. You have to go
for wonder that's simply out there
and wonder that comes from reflection and waiting
or appears to appear coldly from nothing
and quietly ticks in unknown Time.
I'll probably have to learn Italian.
God knows what else I'll have to do.

BEAUTY

We have opinions about beauty,
whether something should be even
or jagged, or if a strangeness needs
to be in it. I haven't preferred
the kind of beauty that's lush, and I'm glad
the bohemian thing never appealed
to me, people earnestly trying
to be artistic and bored with the world.
How in the world could the world be boring?
I think beauty's pretty important—
it's good to have ideas about it,
knowing over time they'll change.
And you only need a little beauty
before you notice its effects—
it has a way of lingering
and blowing the clouds out of your mind,
and pretty soon you realize
you're on the road to happiness.
I tend to like a basic beauty,
an inherent beauty that surprises,
like a dragonfly that lights on the tip
of a tall cattail leaf
among the other cattails growing
at the edge of a still pond in summer.
I've heard that means a chance of rain—
but there's a chance of everything.
This image was presented to me
today at evening time in the lush
of summer beauty, and the leaf,
so awkwardly tall and skinny, put me
in mind of a man wearing a suit
of green topped with a bow tie
and standing there, as if he had paused
to be reflective in the swale.

The dragonfly was motionless
and the sun was coming down the hill.
The man was green to his neck, but missing,
perhaps symbolically, his head.
I like a beauty that's serene
and mired, to be admired in stillness.
I like a stream of consciousness,
but I prefer a stream of crows
crossing a paling, dusky sky,
or better still, an actual stream
and the noisy beauty of the thing.
And how the light will come down to it,
and then the dark will come down to it.

YELLOW TIME

I'll not describe the field it pleased me
to enter with nothing on my mind
because nothing was what I needed
then at the moment of beginning.
Proximity soon mattered—I looked
at things a small distance away
and tried to keep a radius
of ten to twenty feet around.
I wasn't going for a vista,
I wasn't going for anything
at first—that was the mystical point,
to set out empty hearted and blank
in the brain. I didn't have a thought
for several rounds around the field,
just being methodical and quiet
without a purpose. It was morning,
I was solemn in a happy way.
I was basically walking around a field
with an open heart and an empty mind,
and then there wasn't a heavenly voice
at all, but I saw the yellow yolk
in a daisy's face and it came to me,
it's yellow time, it's yellow time,
as though a gear in the year had ticked.
A lot of yellow was there to see,
it was easy to see it everywhere,
even the grass was tinged with yellow,
yet I had to admit I was wrong. I saw
it's also lavender-purple time,
there were flowers there to tell me so,
if you believe a flower tells.
And so I was admonished, yet drawn
farther into the dream, as if—
as if the prominent yellow flowers

and the lesser lavender-purple ones
had painted me into their scene,
and that's what I was going for.

BLUEBIRD EGG

When life was least inside it, something
whose expertise was native, too,
incapable of plot, came by
to suck the baby's yellow ink
and gently turn the nicked end
of the shell away by placing it
like a prop in the green scene below
the skirt of the peach tree, whose fruit
this year came just to blossom before
a late-arriving, killing frost.
As a work of art the shell is perfect
in form and perfectly deep in blue,
but there is nothing in it now,
and nothing in it now for art.
God allows this snuffing out,
and still I let him be my darling—
it isn't always easy, you God,
who made the birds and trees and death.

THE GARDEN

for Jenna Johnson

I was down there pulling weeds from my patch
and noticed my fingers had all turned green.
I had a green blur at the end
of each arm, and my favorite hue of green,
with brightness in it. It's wonderful
to learn what you can make of yourself,
to see what you become. I think
it happens if you just let life
be life. It'll take you along with it.
I became a man with green hands.
I hadn't thought about it much,
but I'd decided to let life
be life and my life would be inside it.
Why wouldn't I be glad of that?
After I'd gotten good and green,
I raised my arms and held them up
and pretended to be a giant bug
with a green glob at the end of its feelers,
but soon I went back to being a man
with green hands, bent over the patch.
And I knew it was the patch that made me,
the instilling green of the garden patch,
whose rows I'd tried to redefine,
only to be myself defined,
as life led me, being the life—
a green thought in a green shade,
and that is how a world was made.

CHICKEN BRISTLE

There's a place near here called Chicken Bristle.
It's not a very hopeful name,
but it's out in the country and quiet. A handful
of houses are clustered along a lane.
The land is rolling and secret and dark.
My grandmother lived there when she was a girl,
but then it was known as Turnersville—
if you were white. If you were Black,
you lived in Chicken Bristle, Kentucky.
I've seen a map that says the place
is Turnersville, but then a pair
of parentheses has Chicken Bristle
between the crescent moonlike curves.
The curves are like unspoken verses,
and Chicken Bristle is more than a name.
I don't think anyone, Black or white,
prospered there. It was just a place
to live and long and love your people.
It wasn't a place for prospering,
and, anyway, enriching yourself
with simple riches isn't really
prosperity. It's better to know
the land around you is rolling and dark,
pastoral and lulling, and hard.
You set your mind and body to work
and hope the work will reach your heart,
to see, in that repose, some beauty,
some meaning for a human life.
And there you have it, America,
your history in brief. I think
you need to live and long and love
your people. I'm writing this poem while
my daughter sleeps in quiet peace,
only the sound of my pen scratching

its marks on the page, her whistling breath.
It's late in the night. One of these days
I'm going to take her to Chicken Bristle
and hold her up to the air and the wild
and say to her, *Part of you, my love,*
comes from Chicken Bristle, this dark
and lulling place, sprung up like
a thistle patch among the hills.
But isn't it beautiful? Isn't
there sweetness in the very air?

LITTLE DARLING

Sometimes I like to think of a space
that's empty. It could be a room,
but it would just be joists and beams
and wide-plank floors and walls,
a basic structure you could use.
I imagine something stark in a room
like that. I like putting something
in an empty space to see how it fits,
to see if the space defines it more
or if the thing can clarify
the space. In a room one time I leaned
a Little Darling washboard against
a wall. It was the only thing
in the room and conveyed a lot by being
alone in the space, and the space itself
had purpose—it helped to haunt the thing,
it's as if a spirit was in the space,
a spirit stamped with Little Darling
on the board, before the ribs began.
I also like to think of a space
that's outside, a glade surrounded by trees
with a yellowish-green light glowing
in the leaves. The most beautiful thing
I've imagined in the glade is a cradle
with blue flowers blooming like
a blue cloud around it. There's someone
asleep in the cradle, very glad
to be alive in the beautiful world.
For the moment she is wordless and sleeping
and the birds in the trees are singing her deeper
to sleep and the breeze causes the light
from the leaves to dance across her face.
If I can think of anything
more beautiful to put in a glade

I'll be glad to share it with the world,
but I've been dreaming of this scene
for most of my life. When I close my eyes
I see her sleeping in the glade,
I see her cradle in the green.

VIOLETS IN THE FALL

A gang of crows was chasing off
a hawk. The little stream was laughing
and shushing itself. The hawk's reflection
briefly blurred a pool of water
and then the pool went back to waiting
for nothing or the next reflection.
The maple trees were yellow and red,
but redder farther up the stream.
I wanted especially to share
the cloud of redder leaves upstream
with the little girl I had with me,
but she was sleeping. Walking home,
I thought the willow trees around
the pond were standing up like brooms
to sweep the sky. That was the voice
in my head describing the willow trees
as brooms, a thought to stop the world
for a moment's moment. She might have thought
the willows looked like lashes winking
around a deep-green eye,
but as I say, she was asleep
for this excursion in the world.
And she hasn't told me yet about
the voice inside her head. For the moment
that voice is learning how to listen
to its own mysterious silence. I expect
it's like a sanctuary in there
with a candle glowing at the back of the room
and violets dotting the grass outside.

FROG EYES

An old man told me once
if you shake a jar of moonshine
and two bubbles roll together
at the brim of the jar, it proves what's in
the bright realm below is the kind
of shine you'll want to drink in small,
judicious sips. He called the bubbles
that roll together *frog eyes,*
and shook the jar he had to show me.
It's a very accurate description,
yet there's something upside down in
the image, which is the rest of the frog,
stuck to a heaven out of view.

I noticed once peering down from
a branch a pair of raindrops
and even saw reflected in them
upside down the little blur
of the world they captured—black branches
and the blank, silent speck of distance
reaching back beyond the blur.
Two tiny drops to see
and see inside, yet tinier
in each, a world turned upside down
and the scarecrow figure that was me,
and green-gray peeping frogs,
not birds, were singing from the tree.

At the top of a page in the book of Judges
there's a gloss, italicized, that says,
The Levite takes a concubine.
The matter-of-factness startled me.
So I read the passage and several chapters
after. Countless people die,
cities burn to the ground, a war
is going on. The Levite never
has a name, nor does his concubine.
She is ravished—symbolically
I hope. She dies symbolically,
and the Levite symbolically divides

her body and sends her through the land.
People flee to the wilderness
and go up in the mountains. It's hard
to know how much of this is true,
it's partly unbelievable—
it's like a fable, but I think
the divided woman symbolizes
something. A grief to share through all
the land, a violence all inherit,
a portion for all the people of God.
The anonymity I believe,
and all the land, I believe that, too.

CANEBRAKE LOVE AND WATER

A patch of light in the sky appeals,
while a barn owl presides
from the top of the sycamore beside
the stream on its way to enter another.
Confluences of small degree,
a fiddle tune in a minor key—
the rhyme occurs, naturally.
I observe the dim silhouettes,
the continuous reality
of morning when some are still asleep,
the barely seen and the quietly heard.
Love renews itself and keeps
beginning, as water waters the stream
and the stream's entrancing motion is stirred.

This portion of the world is like
a mind with the strains of a song in it,
allowing an inconclusive thought.
None of this needs to be finished now,
but I've enjoyed imagining
the canebrake following
the stream in still serenity,
a stiff presence pricking the air
for what was here originally,
in blades of green and greenish-yellow,
the living thing in the living shadow—
but none of this needs to be finished now.
An art with something quiet in it,
and something that isn't even there.

MAD-FACE MACLEISH

A thought or two about a thing
I find curious and admire
from a great distance—you could say
from the distance of ignorance. Being
not-in-the-know is sometimes pleasant.
That can apply to many things,
but I'm talking about painting. I like
to look at paintings even though
as a heathen my mouth hangs open
in front of one. I like to see
what someone can imagine, what
the mind can do, and then how the mind
teaches the hand to move in tiny
motions. It's like seeing the quilt
and then seeing closer the stitches—
very true in a crazy quilt—
the single leaf defining the tree.
But I can't get it in my head
why so many people in paintings
are looking out with a mad face.
This is especially true of men
from the Renaissance who were dukes and earls.
Who wants to live hundreds of years
with a mad face staring back
from the dead world? Eternally mad—
it's strange to capture that in art.
But the Renaissance was short on fun,
people were learning things and also
dividing up the world and sailing
their big ships into history.
It's caused me to wonder why they bothered
with the mad-face routine? Maybe
the mad face was just in fashion—
people who weren't that powerful

could have the look of importance if
a person had a gigantic painting
of himself with a big mad face.
The look of tenderness was later,
I guess. But I don't really know.
The look of someone falling asleep
on dewy, blue-green grass.
On a similar note, I can't explain
the presence of a thick collection
of poems I have by the late Ameri-
can poet Archibald MacLeish.
The book with a faded purple cover
is just sitting there on the shelf.
I've read it in nibbles, but some
of the longer poems, I confess,
I haven't gotten to. MacLeish
is practically a fossil, an old
idea of what poetry
could be, that, in its time, was new.
But now it sounds tattered and stiff,
a little forced and unconvincing.
He was trying too hard to be a poet.
A lesson there in falling short,
and falling shorter and shorter in time.
But the man had a warm, human spirit,
and I admire it. He thought the world
was going to change. He believed in art.
But it's hard to notice lasting art
in the kingdom of immediacy—
that's how I think of the world sometimes,
although I cringe to hear it—the kingdom
of immediacy. It's just a pose,
the clang of something bitter to say,
it's like a mad face staring
out of the poem. I believe
in art, but only to a point.

It's a way of being in the world.
There's a freedom in it I enjoy,
and I keep the mad face out
most of the time. But there's freedom, too,
in someone singing herself to sleep
on dewy, blue-green grass
beneath a tree whose upper branches
disappear in fog. That isn't art.
It's pleasant to imagine such
a scene, but I don't think it's art.
It's a sweet little girl I dream
about in my own eternity,
a hope that has come to live in the world,
my part of it at least, my kingdom
of fog and trees and glittering grass.

COLLARDS

Some people plant their collards in rows
for a neat, predictable arrangement.
Others, however—and this is really
the old-fashioned way—will plant
their collards in a jumble. They loosen
a little patch of ground and sling
the seed in a blur all over creation.
All over creation—allowing the mind
to contemplate a vastness is pleasing.
And who would argue with creation?
The result of the old-fashioned way
puts one in mind of a green sea
with a bluish haze above it like
a cloud. It looks as if everything
that is is there, a waist-high
and leafy green eternity.
I like to lose my sense of order
in the green world. That's what I call it.
The green world, it's beautiful.
The distinction between the rows and jumble
is probably a metaphor.
A metaphor for what is the question,
but I'm going to sit on it a while,
give it a little time and see
if something illuminating comes
to mind. Or not. It's strangely refreshing
when nothing illuminating happens.
You stand there in the green world
and it is what it is, nothing beyond
itself, silently existing.
Poetry is always surprising.
Naively I've approached it, thinking
some lofty thought to say, only
to discover silence says it all.

I've written of collard greens before
in a rather humorous little poem.
It's a pretty inexhaustible subject,
no wonder I've returned to it
again, and find that having less
and less to say is where the real
poem on the matter is,
in the bluish haze above the green.
Nothing more to say than that,
but in it is a kind of love,
and poetry relies on love.

PISSING IN THE RAIN

Sometimes when it's really raining
I like to step out on the porch
and take a big old country piss.
It is a wayward thing to do,
for those who are stubborn and sometimes go
through the world unsettled, according to
how one has learned and comes to need.
Not taking the straight path,
being unable, is what I mean.
And the point is not some happiness.
Usually, I wait for dark
and let it go, just listening
to the splattering sound and the sound of the rain.
Pissing, pretending to be rain,
and rain beginning in the heavens.
It is a solemn ceremony.
At first it feels like taunting Heaven,
as a figure in a murder ballad,
but the moment is caught by infinity,
and then Heaven drowns me out.
The loud silence that follows it,
that's what I'm looking for out there.

TRANSLATION

for Loyal Jones

So I came out of my rainy bower
covered with white petals dropped
from a tree. My people long ago
whose milky eyes I still can see
would have said I had a God's plenty
of petals on me, an expression I liked
to hear as a boy because I knew
it pointed out the obvious only
to make it—just like that—completely
something else. But those people are gone
away from the world, so I had to say it
myself, the God's plenty of petals
that fell when the little rain came down
and I happened to be under the tree.
I have no idea what plenty is
to God, but it riddles my heart to know
that someone thought about it once,
probably after a day's work
when he was staring at a lantern
or sitting on a porch to watch
the stars enumerate themselves,
and struggling to find the words
to catch it all, then finding them.

THE HANDLE

In a peaceful pastoral moment, I turned
an iron handle up with a hoe.
I was tending the garden, so to speak,
in early summer swelter, when
the blade of the hoe plinked against
the handle. It was a simple *L*
leaning over the loosened ground
and I looked, I looked at the rusty *L*.
It could have been for anything,
but now it was only a heavy handle.
I could stick it in the world to fill
the disappearing pools of water,
or use it for a miracle
machine to bring a mountain back.
I could turn it to the right to make
the sun go down and turn it left
again if the world wanted daylight.
I held the handle to the sky
to see where it might go, to see
if I could turn it in the world,
but I couldn't use it in the blue.
I had to live with everything
the way it was. So I looked at the handle
in my hand—the hand with an *L* in it,
ironically—and for a moment
it seemed alive, like an old expression.
Then I let it thud into my pocket.
It's just a handle now, but I wanted
to feel the weight of something useless.
It had been for years in the dark ground
and then I turned it to the light.
And then I put it back in the dark,
but that was beautiful to me.

A LITTLE RED BOOK

All is danger in this growth
of being alone and not alone
on the wet redeeming path in the woods
and the wordless study of solitude
that follows the path invisibly.
Whatever is in the mind rattles,
but then it, too, becomes absorbed
after a few unsteady steps,
and stops listening to itself.
So I listen to the world and see it,
but that is the world. Today the world
is raining. I'm not raining myself,
though the sound of fingers strumming a table
in the sky is pleasing to my ear.
Today the world is rainy and grayish
with patches of white. It isn't yet
what it's going to be. The world is always
becoming something else, it won't
be still, and yet, it has the feeling
of being constant, especially
if from a distance you see some hills.
For days and days they seem the same,
remote and rounded and blurrier
the farther you see, and thus more likely
to seem unchanging. Art, I think,
must offer more than mere appearance.
The world is more than mere appearance,
it's vastly more. Try listening
to rain and see what you think. It's like
having a little red book
whose spine is cracked and you crack it open
one more time, and there before you
is something else to think about.
If it has symbolic meaning, it's still

too soon to tell, but you study it,
as if the sun is coming out,
or a long empty pond is filled
and a butterfly that should have been battered
to nothing is rising from the grass.

AN ORCHARD AT THE BOTTOM OF A HILL

for Claudia and Kent

Why don't you try just being quiet?
If you can find some silence, maybe
you can listen to it. How it works
is interesting. I really can't
explain it, but you know it when
it's happening. You realize
you're marveling at apple blossoms
and how they're clustered on the tree
and you see the bees meticulously
attending every blossom there,
and you think the tree is kind of sighing.
Such careful beauty in the making.
And then you think, it's really quiet,
but I am not alone in this world.
That's how you know it's happening,
there's something solemn and wonderful
in the quiet, a slow and steady ease.
Whether the tree is actually sighing
is beside the point. It's better to wonder,
you needn't be precise with quiet,
it just becomes another thing.
It isn't a science, it's an art,
like love, or a dog who's pretty good,
asleep in the grass beneath the tree.

THREE OLD MOUNTAIN WOMEN

They were country beauties in their time,
but I knew them when they were old,
wearing straight dark dresses
below the knee, absolved of passion,
what little there had been, because
the women I'm thinking of, my kin,
were practical. Mothers of children,
the rearing, the little patch of land,
and their continuance—what they
were born to—a hard place, a people.
Above all, they were gardeners,
green down to their being-roots,
and roots in the spreading ground below
their calm countenance, when sitting
in a straight-backed chair. A voice
prompted them to tell a tale
and then they told it plainly, aware,
I sometimes thought, of what effect
hearing the tale would have on me,
but now I think I merely needed
a voice, a voice suspended in the air—
Well, I declare—and together they gave it to me.

THE AGE OF REASON

It almost makes me mad to know
there's a little town in Kentucky called
Brightshade. What kind of person
decides to use an oxymoron
to name a place? The little children
who live in Brightshade now and bother
to think about it must be either
confused or double-minded. But maybe
whoever named it Brightshade
just wanted people to think about
where they were from. A relative
of mine went to Brightshade once
and never came back—he disappeared,
as if he were merely grist ground
between the two stones of the name.
It's been a problem we've learned to live with.
Another relative was called
Uncle Brother—which is not
as complicated as it sounds.
He was the baby, the only boy
among several girls, and born to farm.
He was one of these men described
as ramrod straight. These are things
I like to think about, old men
and what their lives have been and whether
they had some overcoming to do.
Whatever overcoming is.
I've speculated through the years
that probably the Age of Reason
was late to arrive in Kentucky and once
it got here it didn't last long, and clearly,
Brightshade acquired its name
when people were less reasonable
which suited them and gave them something

to talk about from time to time,
and when it comes down to it, what
is humanity after all but people
talking to each other, laughing,
or recalling something tragic that happened,
and letting it swirl away, like a leaf
dropped on a river. I'm okay
with the symbolism of that image,
and see the leaf in the mystery
of how the river carries it,
lovingly, lovingly away.

AN IRON RING FASTENED TO A RAIL IN THE BARN

I've got a banjo six feet long
and a red-handled Barlow knife,
so I've got the credentials, Mister, to do
the things I do. It takes a lot
of figuring and time to do it.
The barn is just an empty church,
a solemn spirit is inside it.
Something was tied to a rail, because
an iron ring is fastened there—
maybe to suffer, I don't know.
A world of art is in front of you,
not always elegant art, but art
that reveals its passion. I've decided
to love the elegant less than I love
the wild, the untamed passionate art.
The blurt and cackle of birds, the look
of a curled-up lower leaf on a tree,
the tree itself from underneath—
the unexpected shadowy shape.
This distance across the hills is something
you can hear, like a voice. It's space and time
and the sky-domed air and objects and trees,
the shapes of living things, the wonder
of everything, the only art.
Even a world that's surreal begins
with the world as it is in plain sight
and mystical for being itself.
And what am I to do, to add
to it my little portion of being?
Whoever heard of a six-foot banjo?
That's like playing a man—but playing a man
or a longish woman is something you have
to do if you're serious about
this art, and I don't mean poetry,

I mean the larger art of being
alive in the world and suddenly seeing
an iron ring and wondering what
was its use, and whether it was an art
or whether suffering was involved.
I've come to believe that art can be
a beautiful, necessary wound,
a piercing of the soul and then,
after a dark time, a joy.

MUMBLETY-PEG

You don't see people whittling like
you used to. It's as if whittling is out,
along with mumblety-peg, the kind
of game some boys would play in a barn
some afternoon. People are tired
of the old Americana stuff,
the hokey scenes on calendars,
the beauty of a cat's-eye marble. And yet,
if you're a whittler all you need
is time, a pocketknife, and a stick
and you're in business. I had a teacher
who made a dog from a bar of soap,
right there in the classroom in front of us.
We marveled how the shape took shape.
I made a fantastical rooster once
from a stick. His comb was out of proportion
to his little body. He wasn't persuasive
as a rooster, but who expects a rooster
to be persuasive anyway?
And my grandfather carved an elephant
from a peach pit. The skill he had
is evident. But I wonder why
he wanted to use something small
to represent something large.
What was going through his mind
in 1920, whenever it was?
In a drawer somewhere I have the knife.
The handle is made from bone and the blades
are worn down to nubs. I used
to use it when I played mumblety-peg.
The old knife is sitting there
in the drawer with some cat's-eye marbles
and a couple of dominoes. I used
to like to hear them click together.
It was a very particular click.

SOUP

I had a few potatoes once
that I'd set aside to use for seed,
but I was hungry and I thought
resourceful, so I cut out the eyes
with an old knife, hoping to save
a few for spring. Left on the board,
jagged and lopped, the potatoes looked
like a map of countries, one split off
from another following some dispute.
I was poor and doing different jobs
back then and dreaming what I might be,
as if what I was were nothing yet,
and I was reading and listening
and going into the woods at night.
The potatoes I cut into smaller chunks
and dropped them into the cook pot
with about a gallon of water, some pepper,
and the little bit of salt I had.
I lit the fire and let it cook,
simmering it for hours. I called
it soup, and I wanted it to last.

DOG-EAR

I'd bent the corner of the page
and folded it over again to be sure,
apparently, I'd never forget
the importance of something there so serene
it needn't wear the cloak of beauty,
so undeniably true it need
not be declared. Then years went by
and I was thumbing through and came
to the doubled-over, dog-eared page.
Whatever from instinct I'd imagined
was there had become encumbered now
with the passage of time. Even the line
I'd made in the margin had dimmed, and the word,
in dimmer capitals, was WOW.

ABOUT THE AUTHOR

Maurice Manning lives with his family on a small farm in Kentucky. He teaches at Transylvania University in Lexington and in the Warren Wilson MFA Program for Writers.

Poetry is vital to language and living. Since 1972, Copper Canyon Press has published extraordinary poetry from around the world to engage the imaginations and intellects of readers, writers, booksellers, librarians, teachers, students, and donors.

WE ARE GRATEFUL FOR THE MAJOR SUPPORT PROVIDED BY:

academy of american poets

THE PAUL G. ALLEN
FAMILY FOUNDATION

amazon *literary partnership*

POETRY FOUNDATION

4 CULTURE

Lannan

the point
envision·enact·evolve

ART WORKS.
National Endowment for the Arts
arts.gov

WASHINGTON STATE
ARTS COMMISSION

A&
OFFICE OF ARTS & CULTURE
SEATTLE

The Witter Bynner Foundation
for Poetry

TO LEARN MORE ABOUT UNDERWRITING
COPPER CANYON PRESS TITLES,
PLEASE CALL 360-385-4925 EXT. 103

WE ARE GRATEFUL FOR THE MAJOR SUPPORT PROVIDED BY:

Richard Andrews and
  Colleen Chartier
Anonymous
Jill Baker and Jeffrey Bishop
Anne and Geoffrey Barker
Donna Bellew
Will Blythe
John Branch
Diana Broze
John R. Cahill
Sarah Cavanaugh
Keith Cowan and Linda Walsh
Stephanie Ellis-Smith and
  Douglas Smith
Mimi Gardner Gates
Gull Industries Inc.
  on behalf of William True
William R. Hearst III
Carolyn and Robert Hedin
David and Jane Hibbard
Bruce S. Kahn
Phil Kovacevich and Eric Wechsler

Lakeside Industries Inc.
  on behalf of Jeanne Marie Lee
Maureen Lee and Mark Busto
Ellie Mathews and Carl Youngmann
  as The North Press
Larry Mawby and Lois Bahle
Hank and Liesel Meijer
Petunia Charitable Fund and
  adviser Elizabeth Hebert
Madelyn S. Pitts
Suzanne Rapp and Mark Hamilton
Adam and Lynn Rauch
Emily and Dan Raymond
Joseph C. Roberts
Cynthia Sears
Kim and Jeff Seely
D.D. Wigley
Barbara and Charles Wright
In honor of C.D. Wright,
  from Forrest Gander
Caleb Young as C. Young Creative
The dedicated interns and faithful
  volunteers of Copper Canyon Press

The pressmark for Copper Canyon Press
suggests entrance, connection, and interaction
while holding at its center
an attentive, dynamic space for poetry.

This book is set in Futura Medium and Iowan Old Style.
Book design and composition by Becca Fox Design.
Printed on archival-quality paper.